The heart-traveller

Sri Chinmoy

My Race Prayers

Ganapati Press

2025 SRI CHINMOY CENTRE

ISBN 978-1-911319-63-4

FIRST EDITION WENT TO PRESS ON 13 APRIL 2025

My Race Prayers

part 1

1

My Lord,
My God-realisation-aspiration
Has been crying for centuries,
And yet I do not know
Where You are
Or where I am.

2

My Lord,
You are commanding me
　To join You
In Your beginningless
World-transformation-task.
Therefore, my heart is all gratitude
　To You.

3

O Lord,
How beautiful is the morning
When I can see Your Beauty's Eye
And Duty's Hands and Legs
Circling the dreaming hopes
  Of my life,
The streaming tears
  Of my heart
And the blossoming smiles
  Of my soul!

4

My Lord Supreme,
My prayers cannot satisfy You.
My meditations cannot satisfy You.
What else, then, can I do for You
　To satisfy You?

"My child,
How do you know
That your prayers and meditations
Are not satisfying Me?
They do satisfy Me.
But I want you to satisfy Me
Sleeplessly and breathlessly,
And infinitely more,
　Infinitely more."

5

When I look into God's Eye,
I see that He is Infinite and I am finite.
When I look into God's Heart,
I clearly see and throbbingly feel
That I am His Eternity's doll
And He is my Eternity's All.

6

My Lord, an unconditionally
God-surrendered seeker
And God-surrendered lover
   Is the beauty
Of the ever-blossoming
Universal Consciousness
   And the fragrance
Of the ever-heightening
Transcendental Consciousness.

7

My Lord, my Lord, my Lord!
My God-discovery has solved
Not only all intricate mysteries,
But also all insoluble problems,
Past, present and future.
My Lord, You have given me
   And I have.

"My child, I have given you
   And you are."

8

My Lord Supreme
Voraciously devours
The beaming smiles
　Of my soul.
My Lord Supreme
Voraciously devours
The streaming tears
　Of my heart.

9

My Lord, my Lord,
The outer runner promises
God-Joy-Manifestation
　On earth.
The inner runner fulfils
　The promise.
The outer runner runs
　For God.
The inner runner runs
　With God.

10

Every morning I gladden
My Lord's Heart immensely
By crying and flying
　In my inner life,
And by smiling and running
　In my outer life.

11

My Lord, my Lord, my Lord,
My running is the rose-beauty
　And jasmine-fragrance
Of my God-blossoming heart.

12

My Lord, my Lord,
You are telling me that
A smiling heart-runner
Is the enjoyer supreme
Of Heaven's infinite Beauty
And immortal Fragrance,
Specially when the runner runs
In inclement weather,
Unpleasant weather,
Uninspiring weather
And undivine weather.

13

My Lord, my Lord,
My implicit faith
In my God-surrender-run
Is speedily and safely
   Taking me
To my God-Destination
Of the ever-blossoming
And ever-heightening Beyond.

14

My Lord, my Lord,
You are reminding me
Again and again
Of the undeniable fact
That a sleeplessly self-giving seeker
Is absolutely the fastest runner
In the worlds of aspiration
  And dedication.

15

I am a morning runner.
  God gives me His Beauty.
I am a midday runner.
  God gives me His Power.
I am an afternoon runner.
  God gives me His Charm.
I am an evening runner.
  God gives me His Peace.
I am a midnight runner.
  God gives me His Pride.

16

O our 3,100-mile-run runners,
My sleepless, prayerful, soulful, powerful
And proud gratitude-heart-throbs
  I have discovered
In your aspiration-mountain-height
And in your dedication-fountain-delight.
O my Saturday two-mile-race runners,
Your running is challenging,
Yet charming and thrilling.

17

My Lord Beloved Supreme,
You have given
My finite gratitude-heart
  The capacity
To bind Your Universal Life
And Transcendental Self
  At the same time.

18

My Lord, my Lord, my Lord!
The Heaven-born fragrance
   Of my inner running-soul
Becomes the earth-transforming beauty
   Of my outer running-life.
My Lord, my Lord, my Lord!

19

My Lord, my Lord,
My morning run unites
My God-readiness-heart
With God's absolute Fulness-Smile.

20

My Lord, my Lord,
When my body, my vital
And my mind walk,
　My name becomes transformation.
When my heart runs,
　My name becomes satisfaction.
When my soul flies,
　My name becomes perfection,
And God tells me who I eternally am.

21

My Lord, my Lord,
My life is my patience.
My patience is God's Satisfaction.
God's Satisfaction is my All
In the inner world
　Of my God-realisation
And in the outer world
　Of my God-manifestation.

22

May every morning
  My life become
The lotus-beauty-fragrance-petals
  Of my God-oneness-heart.

23

This morning God asked my mind
If my mind sleeplessly loves Him.
Then God asked my heart
If my heart breathlessly needs Him.
My mind immediately said to God,
"I definitely love You sleeplessly."
My heart prayerfully said to God,
"My Lord, please give me
  A few years.
Right now I am quite uncertain."
God said to my mind,
"My son, cultivate sincerity!"
God said to my heart,
"My child, develop speed!"

24

Slowly, steadily and unerringly
My earth-life-tree grows,
   Blossoms and glows
Under the Compassion-Vision-Eye
   Of my Absolute Lord Supreme.

25

The mind's greatness-heights
   Are perishable.
The heart's goodness-depths
   Are imperishable.

26

My Lord,
With the beauty
   Of my outer running
And with the fragrance
   Of my inner running,
I shall make my God-manifestation
A must.

27

The outer run inspires me
  To go and see God.
The inner run inspires me
  To come and sit at God's Feet.

28

My Lord,
To love running
In the morning
Is the beginning
Of my God-pleasing life.

29

My Lord,
Not with my earthly skill,
And not with my Heavenly will,
But with my Lord's
Express Arrival-Thrill
I have completely transformed
  My life.

30

In the morning
I am the blossoming beauty of God.
During the day
I am the unending duty of God.
At night
I am the dreaming melody of God.

31

God's golden Touch
  I love.
God's golden Smiles
  I treasure.
God's golden Tears
  I devour.

32

My Lord,
Not the streaming tears
Of the most deplorable defeats,
But the beaming smiles
Of the most laudable victories,
My life and I eternally are.

33

My Lord, I have won
   Your Victory-Face
By running every day
   Your morning Race.

34

My morning run
Shortens my goal.
So says my heart's
Divine blue-gold soul.

35

Because I love God,
   God exists.
Because I need God,
   God smiles.
Because I sing God's Victory-Song,
   God proudly belongs to me.

36

My inner hunger cries;
My life of beauty flies.
My dream-boat-heart sails;
It never, never fails.

37

There is only one victory
In my inner life and outer life,
And that victory is
My self-transcendence
　In God's own Way.

38

My Lord,
Do shower wisdom-light
　Upon me.
In the spiritual run,
Retirement is conscious
Ignorance-bondage-
　Appointment-engagement.

39

Never say that the world is wrong,
But say that the world
   Can be perfected
Slowly, steadily, unerringly
And unmistakably.

40

My Lord,
When I look at Your Feet,
You ask me to look at Your Face.
When I look at Your Face,
You ask me to look at Your Eye.
When I look at Your Eye,
You ask me to enter into Your Heart.
The moment I enter into Your Heart,
You blessingfully and proudly tell me,
   "My child, now you can rest."

41

Light, more light,
Abundant light and infinite light!
　Every day
In our inner life of aspiration
May we observe our festival of lights.

42

Mornings come to me
With the sound-power
　Of the Unknown.
Evenings come to me
With the silence-peace
　Of the Unknowable.
My Lord Beloved Supreme
Comes to me both in the mornings
　And in the evenings
With what He has and what He is:
　Concern.

43

To my greatest joy,
Today I have come to realise
That it is infinitely easier for me
To please my Lord Supreme
　In His own Way
Than to please myself
　In my own way.

44

My Lord,
I have enjoyed the beauty
Of the world.
I have enjoyed the fragrance
Of the world.
What more do I have to do, my Lord?
"My child,
I now want you to become
The streaming tears
And the bleeding hearts
　Of the world
To become My most perfect instrument
　On earth."

45

The pride of the earthly race
And the joy of the Heavenly Race
Have the same goal:
Self-transcendence.

46

Our Lord wants to hear everything
　From our God-union-heart.
Our Lord does not want to hear
Even a single word
　From our God-division-mind.

47

My Lord, my Lord,
Do keep me sleeplessly
Only with the God-necessity-seekers,
And never, never
With those who are self-sufficient.

48

My Lord, You want me to pray.
I pray for Your Compassion-Eye.
My Lord, You want me to meditate.
I meditate on Your Victory-Banner.
My Lord, do tell me
If I am supposed to do anything else.

"Yes, My child,
You have to do something more.
When you are in a bad mood,
Repeat and repeat and repeat,
'My Lord, I am all for You.'
And when you are in a good mood,
Repeat and repeat and repeat,
'My Lord, You are all for me,
　All for me, all for me.'"

49

   Love the world.
Frustration and renunciation
Shall be your two more names.
   Love God.
God's Grace and God's Praise
Shall be your two more names.

50

Surrender, surrender, surrender!
I must surrender my life,
My heart and my very breath
To the Will of my Lord Beloved Supreme
   At every moment.
If I succeed, only then will He claim me
   As His own, very own.

51

My life will be
Of a very, very, very special significance
   Here on earth
If I can be a constantly cheerful
   Self-giver
To the Will of my Lord Beloved Supreme.

52

My Lord, can You not see
That my outer world
Is dark, darker, darkest?

"My child, can you not see
That I have kept your inner world
Bright, brighter, brightest,
Plus pure, purer, purest?"

53

I pray and pray and pray
When my life needs God.
I meditate, I meditate, I meditate
When my heart loves God.

54

No, no, the outer running is not fun.
  It is our heart's joy-invocation.
No, no, the outer running is not fun.
  It is our soul's Godful inspiration.

55

I love my Lord, I love my Lord!
  Therefore I cry and cry.
I need my Lord, I need my Lord!
  Therefore I try and try.

56

My Lord, may I say something to You?
"Yes, My child, yes."
My Lord, I want to be near You.

"No, My child, I want you to say:
'My Lord, I want to touch You.'
No, My child, I want you to say:
'My Lord, I want to catch You.'
No, My child, I want you to say:
'My Lord, I want to embrace You.'
No, My child, I want you to say:
'My Lord, I want to fulfil You.'
No, My child, I want you to say:
'My Lord, I want to surrender
My earth-existence to You.'
My child, then do it!"

My Lord, I am doing it.

"Heaven, look, look! Earth, look, look!
My child has made his unconditional
And complete surrender to Me.
My child, you have now become

The Heart of My Life
And the Breath of My Soul."

57

Victory, Victory,
Our Lord's supreme Victory,
We must proclaim and establish
Here on earth at every moment.

58

Alas, alas,
Our conscious and unconscious pride
  Has completely destroyed
Our long-cherished God-oneness-joy.

59

Devotion, devotion,
Sleepless, breathless God-devotion!
No devotion —
No highest, no higher, no high
God-realisation.

60

I do not want my God-hunger
Only to be a childish hobby.
I want my God-hunger
   To win
God's Satisfaction-Trophy.

61

My Lord, I have seen
The Beauty of Your Eye,
But I have not felt
The Power of Your Heart,
And I have not become
The dust of Your Feet —
Alas, alas, alas!

62

Alas, I cannot remember
The last time when
My heart most sincerely,
Most soulfully and most self-givingly
 Said to God,
"My Lord Beloved Supreme,
I love You only,
And I need You only."

63

In supreme Silence
The Absolute Lord Supreme
Says to the God-Realised souls,
"My supremely chosen children,
I bring you into the world
Not to defend yourselves
Under any circumstances,
But to love Me and serve Me
Unconditionally, sleeplessly
  And breathlessly
In My own Way
In each human being
And also in each earth-planet-creation
  Of Mine.

You must realise that as you claim Me
  To be your All,
Even so, I claim you,
My Oneness-Vision-Reality-children,
  To be My All."

64

   Expectation
Is frustration-poison-drinking.
   A constant self-giving
Is nectar-delight-drinking.

65

My Lord,
I wish to know from You personally
The differences that exist
Between You and me.

"My child,
There are countless differences
But I shall name only three:
Unlike Me, every day
You have a very tight schedule.
You have no time to write to Me.
You have no time to speak to Me.
You do not even have the time
To speak to me over your heart-phone.
I write to you every day.
I try to speak to you every day.

But alas, alas and alas,
I get no response from you.
Now the second difference is this:
I constantly make fun of myself.
Alas, you have not yet learnt
This particular art,
And I have no idea whether
You will ever be able to learn this art.
The third difference is this:
You think and you feel
That you are indispensable
There in Heaven and here on earth.

In My case, I am absolutely sure
That not only this world,
But also all the worlds
That are in existence,
Can live without Me.
In a sense, you are badly needed
Here, there and all-where.
In My case, nobody wants Me,
Nobody needs Me.
I am left all alone."

66

Each God-seeker
Is the Beauty of God's Heart,
The Divinity of God's Breath
And the Immortality of God's Dream.

67

God loves me
Not because I am a very good
   God-seeker.
God blesses me with His Compassion
Not because I am a very bad
   God-seeker.
God loves me and blesses me
Precisely because I am
His Eternity's child-flower
   And
His Infinity's dream-fragrance.

68

The seeker's spiritual life begins
Only when he sincerely feels
That he is only for God,
Only for God, only for God.

69

I must breathe in every Breath
Of my Lord Beloved Supreme
With a tremendous soulfulness,
Eagerness and intensity.

70

I really love
My ever-blossoming
God-manifestation-tears and smiles,
　I really do.

71

Two kings: the inner and the outer.
The outer king prays to the inner King
 For power, boundless power.
The inner King says to the outer king,
"My child, not power,
But light, light, light!"
The outer king says to the inner King,

"My Father Lord Supreme,
How can I be like You?"
The inner King says to the outer king,
"My child, love Me, pray to Me,
Surrender to Me and claim Me.
You are bound to realise that
Who I am and what I am
You already are in the inner world."

72

My morning running prayer
 Is my heart's
  Silence-bliss.

73

Each new morning
Is a new opportunity for me
To sit in a new way
At my Lord's Feet
And devour the dust
Of my Lord's new Feet
In a new way.

74

My outer running shows me
　The smiling Face of God.
My inner running brings me
　The dancing Heart of God.

75

We must not enjoy
Our comfortable way of thinking
　About God.
We must enjoy only
Our self-giving willingness
　To fulfil God's Will.

76

This morning
My Lord Supreme commanded me
 To use His Mirror.
I immediately obeyed His Command.
To my widest astonishment,
I saw myself as a budding God.
I said to my Beloved Supreme,
"What about Your other children?
You have countless children.
What about them?"
Smilingly and blessingfully
He said to me,
"They are also the same, My child.
All your brothers and sisters
Are also budding Gods and Goddesses."

77

Today my life
Has a new name:
Attachment-extinction.

78

My heart
Is my Master's home,
　Only home.
I must not roam,
I must not roam.

79

God tells me
That if I try to hide
From His Compassion-Eye
And His Forgiveness-Heart,
Then He will deliberately forget
My outer name
And my inner home.

80

Today I am in
The seventh Heaven of delight.
　Why?
My heart's devotion-tears
And my life's surrender-smiles
Are playing hide-and-seek.

81

Smiling,
The breath of the New Year
Has just entered into my heart
And has given me
Three spiritual names:
Excitement, enlightenment
  And fulfilment.

82

This morning
My heart was running
With the God-obedience-currents
  And dancing
With the God-obedience-waves.

83

My Lord,
What is more important,
Your Blessings or Your Love?

"My child,
Both are equally important.
My Blessings you need
To make yourself absolutely divine.
My Love you need
   To become
A supremely choice instrument
Of My Transcendental Vision."

84

If you believe that
To please God in His own Way
   Is essential in your life,
Then why not do it immediately?

85

In spite of being
Shockingly undivine,
Human beings pray to God,
Love God and serve God.
This is, indeed,
The greatest miracle of all.

86

My Lord,
You had to wait
Countless years
For me to come and see You.
How is it that I cannot wait
One single, solitary day
For You to come and see me?

"My child,
Awake, arise –
Arise, awake!"

87

A seeker-runner's life
　Is made of
God's Heart-Songs.

88

When I start counting
My Lord's Blessings
Upon my devoted head
And surrendered life,
In no time I fall asleep.
My Lord blesses me
With the sweetest dream.
In that dream I see and hear
　God telling me,

"My child,
You do not have to count
　My Blessings.
You just be happy and remain happy,
Be happy and remain happy.
Your happiness is all I want
　From your inner life
And your outer life as well."

89

The outer world
Is time-bondage-imprisonment.
The inner world
Is Eternity's
Freedom-enlightenment-achievement.

90

Ignorance-night
Is extremely, extremely proud of
　Disobedience-pride.

91

When we pay any attention
To our doubting mind,
Our aspiring heart starves
　And withdraws.

92

My earthly hope says,
  "I can."
My Heavenly promise says,
  "I already have done:
God-fulfilment-assurance
  On the path."

93

The human life
Is for the God-hunger.
The divine life
Is for the universal feast.

94

Run, run, run!
Spirituality needs both
The inner running
And the outer running.
Neither the inner running
Nor the outer running
Is a curiosity-invitation.
In the life of a genuine God-seeker
  And God-lover,
Curiosity-indulgence is an inescapable
And inevitable self-destructive force.
Only when God's unconditional
Forgiveness-Power descends,
Can the seeker make a fresh attempt
At spiritual progress.
Before we accept spirituality,
Curiosity may inspire a certain seeker
To enter into the spiritual life.
But once a seeker is spiritually
  Well-established,
Curiosity-indulgence
Is the most self-destructive force.

95

I am a God-dreamer-life.
I am a God-lover-heart.
I am a God-listener-mind.
I am a God-carrier-vital.
I am a God-server-body.
I am a God-treasurer-soul.
I am a God-whisperer-soul.
I am a God-drummer-soul.
I am a God-messenger-soul.
I am a God-harbinger-soul.

Commentary: How I wish all of you would learn this prayer by heart. It will definitely, definitely help you in your aspiration-life, so all of you kindly learn it by heart. This is a most special prayer. If you can memorise it, I will be so grateful to you.

96

No age will replace
Our Master's tears
And our Master's smiles.

No age will replace
My children's love for me
And their faith in me.

No age will replace
My gratitude to their hearts
And their gratitude to my life.

97

Be brave, be brave, be brave!
Live not in fear-torture-cave.
Be brave, be brave, be brave,
The way to God's Home to pave.

98

My prayerful and soulful service
   To humanity
Is not my sacrifice.
It is the gigantic fulfilment
Of my Heaven-climbing
And God-fulfilling dream.

99

I must transcend my previous
Aspiration-heart-height, I must!
I must surpass my previous
Dedication-life-length, I must!
I must deepen my previous
Ecstasy-soul-depth, I must!

100

The real spiritual life means
Daily, weekly, monthly, yearly
   And eternally
The victory of
Self-transcendence-discovery.

Notes to *My Race Prayers*, part 1

1. 3 December 1999, Curitiba, Brazil.
2. 31 December 1999, Curitiba, Brazil.
3. 8 January 2000, Iguassu Falls, Brazil.
4. 12 January 2000, Iguassu Falls, Brazil.
5. 15 January 2000, Iguassu Falls, Brazil.
6. 19 January 2000, Asunción, Paraguay.
7. 22 January 2000 Asunción, Paraguay.
8. 22 January 2000, Asunción, Paraguay.
8. 27 January 2000, Brasilia, Brazil.
9. 5 February 2000, New York.
10. 26 February 2000, New York.
11. 4 March 2000, New York.
12. 11 March 2000, New York.
13. 18 March 2000, New York.
14. 25 March 2000, New York.
15. 29 April 2000, New York.
16. 29 July 2000, New York.
17. 5 August 2000, New York.
18. 26 August 2000, New York.
19. 16 September 2000, New York.
20. 28 October 2000, New York.
21. 11 November 2000, New York.
22. 2 December 2000, Ayutthaya, Thailand.
23. 20 December 2000, Mandalay, Myanmar.

24. 23 December 2000, Mandalay, Myanmar.
25. 13 January 2001, Bali, Indonesia.
26. 10 February 2001, New York.
27. 17 February 2001, New York.
28. 24 February 2001, New York.
29. 10 March 2001, New York.
30. 17 March 2001, New York.
31. 24 March 2001, New York.
32. 31 March 2001, New York.
33. 7 April 2001, New York.
34. 10 April 2001, New York.
35. 21 April 2001, New York.
36. 28 April 2001, New York.
37. 12 May 2001, New York.
38. 23 June 2001, New York.
39. 30 June 2001, New York.
40. 7 July 2001, New York.
41. 14 July 2001, New York.
42. 21 July 2001, New York.
43. 4 August 2001, New York.
44. 11 August 2001, New York.
45. 25 May 2002, New York.
46. 8 June 2002, New York.
47. 13 July 2002, New York.
48. 20 July 2002, New York.

49. 27 July 2002, New York.
50. 10 August 2002, New York.
51. 1 March 2003, New York.
52. 22 March 2003, New York.
53. 5 April 2003, New York.
54. 17 May 2003, New York.
55. 31 May 2003, New York.
56. 7 June 2003, New York.
57. 14 June 2003, New York.
58. 14 June 2003, New York.
59. 19 July 2003, New York.
60. 26 July 2003, New York.
61. 9 August 2003, New York.
62. 11 October 2003, New York.
63. 25 October 2003, New York.
64. 1 November 2003, New York.
65. 8 November 2003, New York.
66. 15 November 2003, New York.
67. 22 November 2003, New York.
68. 28 November 2003, Singapore.
69. December 2003, Solo, Indonesia.
70. 6 December 2003, Solo, Indonesia.
71. 10 December 2003, Solo, Indonesia.
72. 11 December 2003, Solo, Indonesia.
73. 12 December 2003, Solo, Indonesia.

74. 13 December 2003, Solo, Indonesia.
75. 17 December 2003, Yogyakarta, Indonesia.
76. 18 December 2003, Yogyakarta, Indonesia.
77. 19 December 2003, Yogyakarta, Indonesia.
78. 21 December 2003, Yogyakarta, Indonesia.
79. 24 December 2003, Yogyakarta, Indonesia.
80. 28 December 2003, Yogyakarta, Indonesia.
81. 31 December 2003, Yogyakarta, Indonesia.
83. 7 January 2004, Bali, Indonesia.
84. 14 January 2004, Bali, Indonesia.
85. 17 January 2004, Bali, Indonesia.
86. 21 January 2004, Bali, Indonesia.
87. 22 January 2004, Bali, Indonesia.
88. 23 January 2004, Bali, Indonesia.
89. 25 January 2004, Bali, Indonesia.
90. 27 January 2004, Bali, Indonesia.
91. 28 January 2004, Bali, Indonesia.
92. 29 January 2004, Bali, Indonesia.
93. 31 January 2004, Bali, Indonesia.
94. 21 February 2004, New York.
95. 28 February 2004, New York.
96. 6 March 2004, New York.
97. 13 March 2004, New York.
98. 20 March 2004, New York.
99. 27 March 2004, New York.
100. 3 April 2004, New York.

My Race Prayers

part 2

101

The outer weather challenges us;
The inner weather frightens us.
But our Lord's infinite Compassion,
Affection, Love and Concern
Enable us to silence and smash
Their pride and torture.

102

A self-conquered
And God-surrendered seeker
Is absolutely the best
   God-lover
And the most perfect
   God-server.

103

Each time an unconditionally
God-surrendered seeker
Meets with God,
God tells him,
"My child, you are the beauty
  Of My Soul's
    Transcendental Dream
And you are the duty
  Of My Heart's
    Universal Reality."

104

Today
My Lord's Compassion-Victory
And my life's surrender-victory
We shall together celebrate.

105

My Lord Supreme,
May Thy Victory be proclaimed
In and through me
At every moment of my life.
My Lord Supreme,
My Lord Supreme,
My Lord Supreme!

106

The human life is
A confusion-dissatisfaction-jungle.
The divine life is
A beauty-fragrance-garden.
A God-seeker's sleepless
  God-surrender-life is
A God-Heartbeat-assimilation-
  Experience-delight.

107

Supreme,
My Supreme,
My Lord Supreme,
My Beloved Supreme,
My heart, my life and I
Wish to learn only two things from You:
Do teach us how to cry for You,
   Only for You,
And how to surrender ourselves
Entirely and completely to You,
   Only to You.

108

Those who love God happily,
Cheerfully, self-givingly, unconditionally,
Sleeplessly and breathlessly
Will never, never, never believe
In God's defeat-failures.
To them, every moment is God's Victory,
God's Supreme Victory,
Even though at times
Our wee human mind
Cannot understand the significance
Of God's constant Victory,
Victory Transcendental
And Victory Universal.

109

My outer running
Is my body's journey –
The destination is known.
My inner running
Is my soul's journey –
The Goal is unknowable.

110

The life that does not believe in
God-loving and God-pleasing prayers
Will end in a most painful failure.
The life that believes in
God-loving and God-fulfilling prayers
Will unmistakably grow into
God's brightest Smile and highest Pride.

111

My body unconsciously loves
Harmful silence-lethargy.
My heart consciously loves
Soulful silence-ecstasy.
I consciously plus self-givingly love
Godful silence-intimacy.

112

For God-realisation,
Needed: no outer skill.
Needed, needed, needed:
Only a God-crying thrill.

113

My Lord, my Lord, my Lord!
I am no more
A "give me" beggar.
From now on I shall be
A "take me" child –
Your child.

114

Learn more truth.
Earn more joy.
Be more perfect.
Be more perfect.
Earn more joy.
Learn more truth.
This message-light
Is for all.

115

I give my money-power to God.
God smiles at me.
I give my name, my fame,
My joy and my pride to God.
God smiles at me twice.
I give my oneness-heart
Unreservedly to God.
God smiles at me a million times
And embraces me a million times.
I give my cheerful, sleepless
And unconditional
Surrender-breath to God.
God smiles at me
And deliberately forgets to stop.
God embraces me
And deliberately forgets to stop.

116

The mind thinks
That God is unapproachable.
The heart knows and feels
That God is not only approachable
But also sleeplessly lovable
And breathlessly adorable.

117

Who is my hero?
No, not a good God-talker.
Who is my hero?
No, not a good God-dreamer.
Who is my hero?
No, not a good God-lover.
Who is my hero?
No, not a good God-server.
Who is my hero?
My hero, indeed:
A God-bleeding heart
And a God-blossoming life.

118

I am proud of myself
Because I think of God every day.
God is proud of Himself
Because He thinks of me
At every moment, at each hush gap.
I am proud of myself
Because I love God only.
God says to me,
"Is it so, My child?
Is it so, My child?
I do not think so, My child.
I do not think so, My child."

119

I fly to please my soul.
I cry to please my heart.
I judge to please my mind.
I challenge to please my vital.
I rest to please my body.
I suffer to please my life.
I love, I serve, I serve, I love
To please my Lord Beloved Supreme.

120

Today's marathon is a unique
God-invocation, God-revelation
And God-manifestation-journey
In the physical body-world.

121

Smiling and smiling,
Whispering and whispering,
Singing and singing,
Dancing and dancing,
Our birthdays descend
From the highest Height
Of Delight-flooded Heaven
And stand before us here on earth
To tell us that God wants us to be
His most powerful soldiers
And His choicest children.

122

Smiling and smiling,
Singing and singing,
God says to each and every
Genuine seeker,
"My child,
Nothing can ever equal
Your heart's climbing cries
And your life's blossoming tears."

123

No minute detail
Can escape God's Attention.
Alas, how can my constant
God-ingratitude-heart
Be an exception?

124

Give me no freedom,
Give me no freedom,
My Lord Supreme.
If You really love me,
Then give me no freedom
Even for a fleeting moment.

125

Love God, serve God,
Sail your life-boat, sail!
If not, my mind,
You fool, wait and fail.

126

My soul is sailing
In God's Pride-Boat.
My heart is sailing
In God's Compassion-Boat.
My life is sailing
In God's Forgiveness-Boat.
I am sailing
In God's Dream-Boat.

127

I place my earthly thoughts
　At God's Feet.
I place my Heavenly will
　Inside God's Heart.
I place myself
　In front of God's Eye.

128

Today I shall break open
My life's ignorance-prison-cell
And ring and ring, sleeplessly ring,
My Lord's Summit-Victory-Bell.

129

When the morning begins,
I sing my Lord's Victory-Song
　Inside my heart.
When the evening sets in,
I strike my Lord's Victory-Gong
Here, there and all-where
　Around the world.

130

My Supreme, my Supreme, my Supreme,
Why do I refuse Your unconditional
Love, Affection, Sweetness and Fondness,
　Why?
My Supreme, my Supreme, my Supreme,
Why do I not sleeplessly and breathlessly
Cry for You,
　Why?
My Supreme, my Supreme, my Supreme,
Why do I not cheerfully give You
What I have and what I am,
　Why?
"Because, because, because, My child,
You have made yourself
The absolute lord of your life."

131

I tried to become great.
God laughed at me.
I tried to become good.
God laughed at me.
I tried to become perfect.
God laughed at me.
Finally I said to God,
"My Lord, I shall become
What You want me to become."
My Lord smiled at me and said,
"My child, now you are truly Mine,
And I am all yours."

132

The outer run
And the inner run
Are two complementary souls.
They help each other
Tremendously.

133

My Lord says to me,
"My child,
Be not a beggar
Of what I have.
Be a chooser
Of who I am."

134

Every morning
God wants my aspiration-heart
And my dedication-life
To run together,
Side by side,
Towards the self-same Goal.

135

My Lord,
How I wish I could tell You
How much I love You!
"My child,
How I wish I could tell you
How much I need you!"

136

My God-running legs
Have made my life
Very precious.
My God-running heart
Has made me
Very gracious.

137

My Supreme has chosen
My heart's streaming tears
To be His Eternity's playmate.

138

My Supreme, my Supreme, my Supreme,
   I love You
Not because You love me infinitely more.
   I love You
Because Your Feet are my only Treasures,
Your Eye is my only Delight
And Your Heart is my only All,
   Only All, only All.
My Supreme, my Supreme, my Supreme!

139

My Lord, my Lord, my Lord,
I am happy, I am happier, I am happiest
Only when I feel that
I am Your bond-slave.

140

I think of You, God.
God says to me, "No good, no good."
I pray to You, God.
God says to me, "No good, no good."
I meditate on You, God.
God says to me, "No good, no good."
I love You, God.
God says to me, "No good, no good."
I serve You, God.
God says to me, "No good, no good."
I surrender to You, God.
God says to me, "No good, no good."
I am all gratitude to You, God.
God says to me, "No good, no good."
I claim You, God, as my own, very own.
God, You claim me as Your own, very own.
God says to me, "Good, good, very good,
My child, My child!"

141

My Lord, my Lord, my Lord,
Never, never take a leave of absence.
My heart and I shall die, die, die
   Immediately.

142

Sorrow, sorrow, sorrow, sorrow,
Every day my heart-field
   You harrow.
But before my earth-life is done,
I shall devour God's Nectar-Sun.

143

Hope, hope, my hope,
Do not desert me!
Continue to nurture
My life-tree.

144

Life and death,
Life and death,
Life and death.
Death and life,
Death and life,
Death and life.
Life conquers death
To sing and play and dance
With the ever-blossoming Beyond.
Death conquers life
Not to torture, but to treasure
The beauty of life's heart
And the fragrance of life's soul.

145

When God says yes,
My heart says yes.
When God says no,
My heart says no.
Only then my God-oneness-life
Blooms and blossoms,
And God claims me
As His own, own, own –
Very own.

146

My outer journey cries and smiles.
My inner journey blooms and blossoms.
And I am the hope-promise-journey
   Of Eternity.

147

Every day I feed
My Inner Pilot
With my complete and constant
Surrender to His Will.

148

Before I start my running,
My Lord looks into my eyes
And smiles and smiles.
After I end my running,
I look at my Lord's Feet
And smile and smile.

149

God the Flute-Heart
  I love.
God the Thunder-Eye
  I need.

150

I race, I race, I race, I race
To be my Supreme's boundless Grace.
I race, I race, I race, I race
To see my Supreme's golden Face.

151

God does not want anyone
To fall and roam.
He wants all His children
To live in His Heart-Home.

152

Do not give up hope,
Do not give up hope!
Hope will give you
A Heaven-climbing rope.

153

My life is full of God-Blessings.
My heart is full of God-Songs.
My mind is full of God-Stories.
My vital is full of God-Flames.
My body is full of God-Dreams.
My thoughts are made of God's Will.
  I am in thrill,
  I am in thrill,
  I am in thrill!

154

My Lord,
Your Sun-Fire-Eye
   Frightens me,
Your Moon-Sweetness-Heart
   Enlightens me
And Your Thunder-Kick-Feet
   Liberate me
From the ignorance-world-night.

155

Peace I need to see the Face
Of my Absolute Lord Supreme.
Bliss I need to sail and fly with Him
And breathe and be His Dream.

156

Every morning
My devotion-heart offers
Streaming gratitude-tears
To my Lord Supreme
And devours the golden dust
Of His golden Feet.

157

My heart runs
The world's longest race,
And not my mind.
My Lord runs ahead of me;
My breath runs behind.

158

Every morn and every eve
My heart and I sing
A new Golden Shore-song.
With twinkling eyes
And dancing heads,
The cosmic gods
And goddesses throng.

159

Let me be good.
Let me be self-giving and pure.
My Supreme Lord's express Arrival
   Shall then be sure.

160

My Lord Supreme, I am praying to You
To bless all the marathon runners
With Your sweet and fond Marathon-Love.
My Lord, they desperately need
   Your Compassion.
My Lord, I am also praying to You
To bless our self-giving organisers.
Self-giving is the right word, my Lord.
They always serve You lovingly
   And self-givingly,
And at times sleeplessly.

My Lord, I am also praying to You
To bless profusely the helpers
And also the well-wishers
   Of this marathon.
May all the runners run
   Smilingly and happily
While covering the entire distance.

161

O my rainbow-heart-sky,
   In you I see
The beauty of the Unknowable,
   In you I feel
The silence of the Unknowable.

162

The outer run has a destination.
The inner run knows no destination.
The inner run is a run of the Beyond,
For the ever-transcending Beyond.
The outer run asks me who I was.
My answer: I was a God-dreamer.
The inner run asks me who I am.
My answer: I am a God-lover.
Finally, God asks me who I would like to be.
My answer: My Lord, I would like to be
Your Eternity's server-slave.
My Lord says, "No, not correct!
I would like you to be the co-pilot
Of My Eternity's Golden Boat-Journey."

163

My Lord, please forgive me.
Today I do not have any special prayer
To place at Your Feet.

"My child, tomorrow you must pray to Me
More than usual."

My Lord, today I am unable to think of You.

"My child, tomorrow you must think of Me
Much more than usual."

My Lord, today I am unable to love You.

"My child,
Tomorrow you must and must and must
Love Me infinitely more
Than you usually do.
My child, today I am forgiving you,
But you must not be negligent
   In your prayers.
You must not be negligent
   In thinking of Me.

You must not be negligent
  In loving Me.
If you want to claim Me to be yours
And if I want to claim you to be Mine,
Then you must never, never, never
Forget your morning spiritual
Love-devotion-surrender-disciplines."

164

No more my life will walk along
A God-empty road.
I am now blossoming
With a lifelong
  God-Touch-Smile,
I am now blossoming
With a lifelong
  God-Touch-Song,
And I am now blossoming
With a lifelong
  God-Touch-Embrace.

165

Not true:
God thinks of me only one time
　During my entire life.
God thinks of me
　All the time.

Not true:
God loves me only one time.
God loves me
　All the time.

Not true:
God needs me only one time.
God needs me
　All the time.

Not true:
God highly appreciates me
　Only one time.
God highly appreciates me
　All the time.

Not true:
God wants me to be another God
   Only for a fleeting day.
God wants me to be another God
   For Eternity.

166

My God-gratitude-heart
Blooms and blossoms
In my soul-beauty's
Heaven-plenitude-smiles.

167

My Lord,
You have given me Your own Eye
　To see the world.
You have given me Your own Ears
　To hear the world.
You have given me Your own Heart
　To love the world.
You have given me all that You have
And all that You are
　To give to the world.
My Lord,
Do give me one more thing.
Please, please give me Your own Feet
To worship You
　Sleeplessly and breathlessly,
My Lord, my Lord.

168

Every morning God comes down
From His highest Heaven
To bless my climbing
  Aspiration-heart-flames
With His Infinity's
  Peace-Bliss-Heart.

169

Every day a new morning angel
Wakes me up to celebrate
  God's Birthday
By clasping God's Eye,
  Embracing God's Heart
    And worshipping God's Feet.

170

When I think of God,
God says to me,
"I am not fully satisfied with you."
When I pray to God,
God says to me,
"I am not fully satisfied with you."
When I meditate on God,
God says to me,
"I am not fully satisfied with you."
When I say to God,
"My Lord, I love You only
And I need You only,"
God says to me,
"My child, come to Me
And be with Me
All the time, all the time."

171

My Supreme,
Out of Your infinite Compassion
You have bound Yourself
Tight, very tight, in the finite
So that we can love You,
Catch You, embrace You
And become Your choice instruments
  Here on earth,
My Supreme!

172

God loves me most dearly.
Therefore, He examines me,
He judges me
Constantly and severely.

173

My Lord,
Be pleased to pour more and more
Your Wisdom-Light
Into the mind of the seekers –
To smile at the morning beauty's sun
And continue smiling during the day
To please You in a very special way.

174

The morning hope-beauty blesses
　The morning runners.
The evening peace-fragrance blesses
　The evening runners.
The outer morning runners
And the outer evening runners
Are helping considerably
Their inner runners' aspiration,
Dedication and manifestation.

175

My Lord,
This morning You are asking me
To join Nature
In her prayer to You:
"My Lord,
You have given me
Beauty infinite,
But You have not given me
My duty."
"My child,
Your duty
Is to climb up incessantly
  To clasp My Feet
And devour the golden dust
  Of My Feet."

176

My Lord, my Lord!
In Your Compassion-flooded Eye
I have discovered my All.

177

My Lord,
You want me to run every day.
Do You ever run?
"My child,
I run not only every day,
But also at every moment.
Do you know why?
I run constantly
From one end of My creation
To the other end.
If I do not run ceaselessly,
My creation will become inactive,
Inert and uselessly idle.
At every moment I run
To awaken and energise
My entire creation."

178

My Supreme,
I wish to see You
Either in my heart's happiness
Or in my life's soulfulness.
This is my most sincere prayer
To You, my Supreme!

179

No more self-indulgence,
No more self-indulgence!
I shall run outwardly
To see Nature's God.
I shall run inwardly
To see Heaven's highest Height.
No more self-indulgence,
No more self-indulgence!

180

Every kneeling prayer
Receives God's
Fondness-Blessings.

181

I have given God what I have:
　The tears of my heart.
God has given me what He has:
　The Smiles of His Eye.
But alas,
One thing we have not been able
To give to each other:
Satisfaction, mutual satisfaction.

182

Today's runners:
Brave you are,
Daring you are,
Weather-defying you are,
God-loving you are,
God-fulfilling you are.
Spirituality braves all obstacles
And then it receives
The Victory-Garland from God.

183

Early in the morning
When we offer
Our pure love to God,
  We do the good thing.
And when we offer
Our pure devotion to God,
  We do the better thing.
Finally, when we offer
Our pure surrender to God,
  We do absolutely by far
    The best thing.

184

The early morning running
Is the God-pleasing
And God-fulfilling dedication
Of the body, vital, mind and heart.

185

Human life is a series
Of inner and outer battles.
Running, jumping, throwing,
Sports and physical fitness
Help us win the outer battles.
Prayers, meditations
And our surrender to God's Will
Help us win the inner battles.

186

I admire God the Dreamer.
I adore God the Smiler.
I love God the Runner.

187

Each time we prayerfully, soulfully
  And self-givingly run,
We make a most serious commitment
  To our God-manifestation-task.

188

The celestial beauty and fragrance
  Of the early morning
Adorn the hearts
Of all God-loving and God-serving
  Children-runners.

189

My outer success gives my Lord
  Immense joy.
My inner progress gives my Lord
  Immeasurable joy.

190

Every morning
God the Hope blesses my life,
God the Promise blesses my heart,
God the Will-Power blesses me.

191

Earth knows only one name:
  Suffering.
Heaven knows only one name:
  Joy.
My soul knows only one name:
  Light.
My heart knows only one Name:
  Lord.
My mind knows only one Name:
  God.
My life knows only one Name:
  Pilot, my Inner Pilot.
And I know only one Name:
  Supreme, my Absolute Supreme.

192

My Lord,
Do give my heart the strength
  To love You most intensely.
My Lord,
Do give my life the strength
  To need You most sincerely.
My Lord,
Do give my legs the strength
  To run most speedily.
My Lord,
Do give me the strength
  To manifest You here on earth
    Most unconditionally.

193

With the smiles of my soul
And the tears of my heart,
I have made a most beautiful
And fragrant garland,
And I am now placing it
At the Feet of my Lord Supreme.

194

God says to my prayers,
"My children,
I love your sincerity and purity."
God says to my meditations,
"My children,
I love your tranquillity and immensity."
God says to me,
"My child,
I love your outer regularity
And your inner punctuality."

195

Alas,
Because of our teeming self-doubts,
The intense and immense joy
Of our morning hearts
Cannot come to the fore
And bloom and blossom.

196

Morning is the best time
To enter into my rose-garden-heart
　To enjoy deeply
Its exquisite beauty and fragrance.

197

To talk about God
Is infinitely easier
Than to think of God.

To think of God
Is infinitely easier
Than to pray to God.

To pray to God
Is infinitely easier
Than to become one
With God's Will.

198

My sleepless love for God
   Is the beauty
Of my ascending heart
   And the fragrance
Of my descending soul.

199

God's ever-blossoming
   Infinite Beauties
My soul can see.
But God's ever-multiplying
   Infinite Duties
Remain unknowable.

200

The tears of my heart
And the Smiles of my Lord
Play together and sing together
   Sleeplessly.

Notes to *My Race Prayers*, part 2

101. 6 April 2004, New York.
102. 9 April 2004, New York.
103. 10 April 2004, New York.
104. 17 April 2004, New York.
105. 24 April 2004, New York.
106. 8 May 2004, New York.
107. 15 May 2004, New York.
108. 22 May 2004, New York.
109. 5 June 2004, New York.
110. 12 June 2004, New York.
111. 26 June 2004, New York.
112. 3 July 2004, New York.
113. 10 July 2004, New York.
114. 17 July 2004, New York.
115. 24 July 2004, New York.
116. 31 July 2004, New York.
117. 7 August 2004, New York.
118. 14 August 2004, New York.
119. 21 August 2004, New York.
120. 25 August 2004, New York.
121. 28 August 2004, New York.
122. 4 September 2004, New York.
123. 11 September 2004, New York.
124. 18 September 2004, New York.

125. 25 September 2004, New York.
126. 9 October 2004, New York.
127. 16 October 2004, New York.
128. 30 October 2004, New York.
129. 6 November 2004, New York.
130. 13 November 2004, New York.
131. 20 November 2004, New York.
132. 13 December 2004, Xiamen, China.
133. 23 December 2004, Qingdao, China.
134. 26 December 2004, Qingdao, China.
135. 30 December 2004, Qingdao, China.
136. 2 January 2005, Qingdao, China.
137. 9 January 2005, Qingdao, China.
138. 19 February 2005, New York.
139. 26 February 2005, New York.
140. 5 March 2005, New York.
141. 12 March 2005, New York.
142. 19 March 2005, New York.
143. 26 March 2005, New York.
144. 2 April 2005, New York.
145. 9 April 2005, New York.
146. 16 April 2005, New York.
147. 23 April 2005, New York.
148. 30 April 2005, New York.
149. 30 April 2005, New York.

150. 6 May 2005, New York.
151. 11 June 2005, New York.
152. 18 June 2005, New York.
153. 9 July 2005, New York.
154. 16 July 2005, New York.
155. 23 July 2005, New York.
156. 30 July 2005, New York.
157. 6 August 2005, New York.
158. 13 August 2005, New York.
159. 20 August 2005, New York.
160. 25 August 2005, New York.
161. 28 August 2005, New York.
162. 3 September 2005, New York.
163. 24 September 2005, New York.
164. 1 October 2005, New York.
165. 22 October 2005, New York.
166. 29 October 2005, New York.
167. 5 November 2005, New York.
168. 12 November 2005, New York.
169. 19 November 2005, New York.
170. 30 November 2005, Pangkor Island, Malaysia.
171. 3 December 2005, Pangkor Island, Malaysia.
172. 7 December 2005, Pangkor Island, Malaysia.
173. 9 December 2005, Pangkor Island, Malaysia.
174. 14 December 2005, Kuantan, Malaysia.

175. 17 December 2005, Kuantan, Malaysia.
176. 21 December 2005, Kuantan, Malaysia.
177. 24 December 2005, Kuantan, Malaysia.
178. 28 December 2005, Kuantan, Malaysia.
179. 31 December 2005, Kuantan, Malaysia.
180. 2 January 2006, Kuantan, Malaysia.
181. 5 January 2006, Kijal, Malaysia.
182. 7 January 2006, Kijal, Malaysia.
183. 11 January 2006, Kijal, Malaysia.
184. 14 January 2006, Kijal, Malaysia.
185. 18 January 2006, Kijal, Malaysia.
186. 21 January 2006, Kijal, Malaysia.
187. 1 February 2006, Penang, Malaysia.
188. 5 February 2006, Penang, Malaysia.
189. 8 February 2006, Penang, Malaysia.
191. 18 February 2006, Langkawi, Malaysia.
192. 23 February 2006, Langkawi, Malaysia.
193. 4 March 2006, New York.
194. 11 March 2006, New York.
195. 18 March 2006, New York.
196. 25 March 2006, New York.
197. 1 April 2006, New York.
198. 9 April 2006, New York.
199. 15 April 2006, New York.
200. 22 April 2006, New York.

My Race-Prayers

part 3

201

O my blue-gold heart-bird,
I love you,
I need you,
I treasure you.
You are my joy,
You are my pride,
You are my All.

202

I love my Lord's
Whisper-Blessings.
My Lord loves my
Hunger-yearnings.

203

Long before God comes to us,
He sends His angels to us.
Before His angels come to us,
God sends us divine thoughts
  And divine feelings.
Before the divine thoughts
  And divine feelings,
He gives us purity-hearts.
With purity we all must begin
  Our spiritual journey.

204

My Lord says to me,
"My child,
Take your outer pain
As your inner gain.
Take your outer failures
As your inner triumphs.
Take your outer life
As an experience.
Take your inner life
As your path-finder."

205

Heaven's Silence-Music
Is only for the hearts
Of God's Victory-singers.

206

In my aspiration-life,
My Master-obedience
Is my heart's
God-blossoming dawn.

207

Only one attachment:
God's Will.
No other attachments,
Old or new!

208

My Lord,
I run and run and run and run
To make You happy.
"My child,
You are the smile of My Eye,
You are the beauty of My Heart
And you are the pride of My Life."

209

Krishna, my Lord,
Your morning flute
Feeds my heart.
Your twilight cows
Feed my eyes.

210

The outer rain
Proudly comes down
From the expansion-sky.
The inner Rain
Blessingfully descends
From God's Compassion-Eye.

211

I have three indispensable Saviours:
My Lord's lavishing Hand,
My Lord's cherishing Heart,
My Lord's protecting Eye.

212

I am the world's longest distance
Daring and shattering runner –
My Supreme Lord's Sun-Power-Smile
And His Moon-Bliss-Love-winner.

213

My tears and smiles
Sleeplessly feed
God's birthless and deathless
Heart-Hunger.

214

I am happy, only happy,
When I place
My naughty mind
And my haughty head
At God's Feet.

215

To all the marathon runners
I am blessingfully offering
My heart's boundless joy,
Boundless gratitude
And boundless pride, pride, pride.

216

Everything is possible.
In a twinkling
I can clasp God's Eye.
In a twinkling
I can touch God's Feet.
In a twinkling
I can breathe God's Heart.

217

The life that has no goal
Is an utter failure-life.
The life that has a goal
Wins the Smile of God.

218

We love our desire-life
Infinitely more than we love God.
God loves only us,
And never, never, never, never
Our desire-life.

219

I speak to God's
Golden Feet.
God speaks to my
Broken heart.

220

True, true, true,
True, true, true –
A pure thought
Can remain unchallenged
In my aspiration-heart.

221

I pray to God's Eye
　For love.
I pray to God's Heart
　For devotion.
I pray to God's Feet
　For surrender.

222

First you must bask
In the sunshine
Of your Master's grace
Before you can see
God's Face.

223

I pray to God
To see His golden Feet.
I meditate on God
To be His choice instrument.

224

While running,
I feel God's Love,
God's Joy and God's Pride
Inside my heart
At every moment.

225

The outer sun
Sadly tells me
How far I am from God.
The inner sun
Secretly tells me
How close I am to God.

226

A self-giving thought
Is a God-fulfilling
Achievement-joy.

227

The outer running
Is the God-awareness-joy.
The inner running
Is the God-closeness-ecstasy.

228

My Lord, my Lord!
In Heaven I adore
Your dreaming Eye.
My Lord, my Lord!
On earth I worship
Your protecting Feet.

229

Down I bring my Lord
  To earth
To cry with me
And weep with my heart.
Up my Lord carries me
  To Heaven
To dream with Him
For a new creation.

230

My life is a humble
Earth-builder.
My heart is an eager
Heaven-promoter.

231

In secrecy supreme
My Beloved Lord tells me
That I have done extremely well
In all my love-devotion-surrender
  Examinations.

232

My eyes can fool me,
My ears can fool me,
But not my heart
That loves God only.

233

Every morning and every evening
My soul, my heart and I
Salute and salute and salute
Our Lord's Victory-Banner.

234

Not God's Kindness,
Not God's Strictness,
But God's Heart-Tears
Have changed my life completely.

235

My Lord,
Do tell me the secret of secrets:
How I can please You all the time
In Your own Way.
"My child,
Sing, sing and sing
Only surrender-songs."

236

Running early in the morning
With God-devotion-heart-joy
Is absolutely the best way
　To start the day.

237

My Lord Supreme,
May I bask every morning
　In the Sunshine
Of Your Heaven-born Smiles.

238

My Lord, my Lord, my Lord,
You live inside my painful body.
You also live inside my blissful heart.
Which place do You prefer?
"My child,
I have no preference.
I love your body and your heart equally.
I suffer and suffer
With your painful body.
I enjoy and enjoy
Your blissful heart."

239

My Lord,
When I pray, it is all wrong.
When I meditate, it is all wrong.
When I serve, it is all wrong.
My Lord, what can I do?
"My child,
Before you pray,
Ask Me to pray in and through you.
Before you meditate,
Ask Me to meditate in and through you.
Before you serve,
Ask Me to serve in and through you.
Give Me the full responsibility.
You just be the witness.
Watch Me, what I do and how I do it."

240

God's Face I love.
God's Eye I love more.
God's Heart I love much more.
God's Feet I love infinitely more.

241

True, my eyes are empty
   Of God's Face,
But my heart is all
God's blossomed Face.

242

Each running step
Beautifully blossoms
As a divine opportunity
To please God in His own Way
Along His Eternity's Road.

243

My constant upward flight
Solely depends on
My heart's receptivity-depth.

244

In my inner life,
I am a Heaven-climbing cry.
In my outer life,
I am a man-serving tree.

245

My failure-life
  Is painful.
My success-life
  Is delightful.
My progress-life
  Is powerful.

246

I chose God-obedience
  To become
God's Heart-Rose.

247

Fast, faster, fastest
  Go alone.
Every day God will speak to you
  Over the phone.

248

Each God-given responsibility-task
Is a golden opportunity
To please God in His own Way.

249

My sleepless surrender
  To God's Will
Entirely depends on
My unconditional love of God.

250

May my heart
Be the beauty
Of a morning rose-garden.

251

In the morning
I swim in the river
  Of God-aspiration.
In the evening
I swim in the sea
  Of God-surrender.

252

Every morning and every evening
I feed my Lord Supreme
With my soul's beauty,
My heart's sincerity
And my life's simplicity.

253

I love the blossoming Beauty
  Of the morning God.
I love the deepening Peace
  Of the evening God.
I love, I love, I love.

254

This morning my Lord Supreme
Has blessingfully shared with me
His most secret
And most sacred Dream —
The time when this world of ours
Shall be inundated with my Lord's
Peace-Beauty and Peace-Fragrance.

255

My Lord,
Please, please, please
Bless me with a supreme Secret.
"My child,
I do not want you to be great.
I do not want you to be good.
I want you to be Mine, only Mine.
This is My supreme Secret."

256

   I sail
My golden dream-reality-boat
   Between
My God-obedience-life-shore
   And
My God-gratitude-heart-shore.

257

Every morning is the birth
   Of a new hope.
Every day is the birth
   Of a new promise.
Every evening is the birth
   Of a new peace.
Every night is the birth
   Of a new dream.

258

Morning is the sacred time
  To offer the world
My God-happiness-soul.
Morning is the secret time
  To feed
My God-longing heart.

259

My sincere humility-life
  Is God's
Precious utility-joy.

260

I sing for God soulfully.
God sings for me blessingfully.
We'll go on, go on
Through Eternity.

261

When the tears of my heart
Go to my Lord crawling,
My Lord immediately embraces them
With infinite Affection, Love,
Sweetness and Fondness,
And then teaches them
How to sprint
   Faster than the fastest,
How to fly
   Higher than the highest
And how to dive
   Deeper than the deepest.

262

Do not surrender to your fate.
Do not accept your fate.
Love God more and more,
   Unconditionally.
God has two big Ears.
He will transform
Your earth-bound fate
Into the Heaven-free Bliss.

263

God's Eye is my body's
   Protection-Temple.
God's Heart is my life's
   Illumination-Shrine.

264

No lasting defeat,
No lasting failure!
At God's Hour –
Victory, victory!
Now just endure.

265

My Lord does not believe
In my very clever mind-flattery.
He believes only
In my life's world-service-tree.

266

Every morning
And every evening
My soul most devotedly records
The Nectar-flooded Discourses
Of my Lord Beloved Supreme.

267

I must make my heart
A pure God-surrender-song
So that I can strike
God's largest Victory-Gong.

268

Marathon is
An unimaginable joy-experience
Of the heart.
Marathon is
An unbearable suffering-experience
Of the body, the vital and the mind.

[Short talk offered before the marathon:]

I have invoked special Blessings of my Absolute Lord Beloved Supreme for all the marathon runners. Each marathon is an unimaginable joy for the runner's heart. Again, each marathon is an unspeakable torture for the body, the vital and the mind. Our philosophy is to transcend – transcend the physical pain and transcend our previous achievements. My blessings, my love and my gratitude I am offering to each and every runner.

And my special request to you all is this: when you find you are tired, extremely, extremely tired, exhausted, then do not continue, do not continue.

All my love. Start!

269

May I be a morning
Ascending wave of bliss.
May I be an evening
Descending wave of peace.

270

Every day I ply my life-boat
Between
My dreaming soul-shore
And
My crying heart-shore.

271

My Lord Supreme,
No more will You suffer
For my sake.
My life has stopped swimming
In ignorance-lake.

272

Life is a constant battle
Between the human in us
And the divine in us –
And the divine in us
Will ultimately wear
Victory's garland.

273

The fever of the body
Comes and goes.
May my God-love-heart-fever
Remain forever and forever.
The fever of the body
Is torture unbearable.
My God-love-heart-fever
Is rapture unimaginable.

Notes to *My Race Prayers, part 3*

201. 29 April 2006, New York.
202. 6 May 2006, New York.
203. 13 May 2006, New York.
204. 20 May 2006, New York.
205. 27 May 2006, New York.
206. 3 June 2006, New York.
207. 10 June 2006, New York.
208. 11 June 2006, New York.
209. 17 June 2006, New York.
210. 24 June 2006, New York.
211. 22 July 2006, New York.
212. 22 July 2006, New York.
213. 5 August 2006, New York.
214. 19 August 2006, New York.
215. 25 August 2006, New York.
216. 9 September 2006, New York.
217. 23 September 2006, New York.
218. 30 September 2006, New York.
219. 7 October 2006, New York.
220. 14 October 2006, New York.
221. 4 November 2006, New York.
222. 11 November 2006, New York.
223. 18 November 2006, New York.
224. 2 December 2006, Belek, Turkey.

225. 7 December 2006, Antalya, Turkey.
226. 10 December 2006, Antalya, Turkey.
227. 13 December 2006, Antalya, Turkey.
228. 16 December 2006, Antalya, Turkey.
229. 20 December 2006, Antalya, Turkey.
230. 23 December 2006, Antalya, Turkey.
231. 26 December 2006, Antalya, Turkey.
232. 30 December 2006, Varna, Bulgaria.
233. 3 January 2007, Varna, Bulgaria.
234. 6 January 2007, Varna, Bulgaria.
235. 10 January 2007, Varna, Bulgaria.
236. 13 January 2007, Varna, Bulgaria.
237. 17 January 2007, Varna, Bulgaria.
238. 27 January 2007, Cha-Am, Thailand.
239. 31 January 2007, Cha-Am, Thailand.
240. 3 February 2007, Cha-Am, Thailand.
241. 9 February 2007, Chiang Mai, Thailand.
242. 13 February 2007, Chiang Mai, Thailand.
243. 16 February 2007, Chiang Mai, Thailand.
244. 20 February 2007, Chiang Mai, Thailand.
245. 23 February 2007, Chiang Mai, Thailand.
246. 3 March 2007, New York.
247. 10 March 2007, New York.
248. 10 March 2007, New York.
249. 31 March 2007, New York.

250. 7 April 2007, New York.
251. 10 April 2007, New York.
252. 14 April 2007, New York.
253. 21 April 2007, New York.
254. 28 April 2007, New York.
255. 5 May 2007, New York.
256. 12 May 2007, New York.
257. 26 May 2007, New York.
258. 2 June 2007, New York.
259. 9 June 2007, New York.
260. 23 June 2007, New York.
261. 7 July 2007, New York.
262. 14 July 2007, New York.
263. 21 July 2007, New York.
264. 28 July 2007, New York.
265. 4 August 2007, New York.
266. 11 August 2007, New York.
267. 19 August 2007, New York.
268. 24 August 2007, Rockland Lake State Park, New York.
269. 26 August 2007, New York.
270. 1 September 2007, New York.
271. 8 September 2007, New York.
272. 15 September 2007, New York.
273. 29 September 2007, New York.

My Blessingful and Pride-Flooded Dedication to the Indomitable Runners of the 3100-mile Self-Transcendence Race, 2006

1

I know
How to run and run
  And run.
My Lord Supreme
  Knows
How to love me
  With His
Blessing-Pride.

2

I run the world's
  Longest Race
To dine with God's
Boundless Grace.

3

  History's
Longest Run-Race
  Is God's
Smile-blossomed Face.

4

The world's
Longest distance-runners
Are God's
  Heart-treasured
    Children.

5

Each
Longest distance-runner
Is a very special
Affection-wave of
  God.

6

The real Name
Of God is Blessing.
  The real Name
Of God's Heart
  Is Love.
The real Name
Of God's Life
  Is Concern.

7

   When
We talk to God,
We show our greatness.
   When
God talks to us,
He gives us His Goodness.

8

Earth-servers
   Are
God's Heart-Climbers.

9

   Each
Self-giving thought
   Is a
Rainbow-Beauty.

10

God's Eye
  Is God's
Sleepless Compassion
  For
His aspiring children.

God's Heart
  Is God's
Breathless Concern
  For
His serving children.

11

  Each
Longest distance-runner
  Is
God's special
  Prize-winner.

12

Prayer is our
Mountain-climbing
  Pride.
Meditation is our
Fountain-enjoying
  Heart.

13

  A
God-rising life
  Is a
God-shining
  Heart.

14

My God-dependence
Is the Beauty
Of my life.

My God-dependence
Is the Fragrance
Of my heart.

15

Running dedication
Knows no enjoying
  Vacation.

16

To-day
My mind is
Utterly absent
Of self-doubt.

17

  I
Wish to have
A new name:
God-dedication-heartbeat.

18

My life-boat plies
   Between
My God-invocation-heart
   And
My God-dedication-life.

19

My only Paradise
   Is my
God-aspiration-heart-garden.

20

Every day
I feed on my Lord's
Compassion-Eye-Beauty.

21

My Earth
Tells me:
 "I can."
My Heaven
Tells me:
 "I am."

22

Earth-mind
Proudly thunders.
Heaven-heart
Sweetly whispers.

23

I need
A new heart
To love God more.
I need
A new life
To need God more.

24

Each
New day
Is flooded
  With
Rainbow-opportunities.

25

The world's
Longest distance runner
Has at once won
God's Compassion-Eye
  And
God's Protection-Heart.

26

My mind wants
God's Power-Tower.
My heart needs
God's Peace-Sea.

27

I do not
Measure God's
Blessingful gifts.
I only treasure
　Them.

28

God prepares
The souls for the earth.
God prepares
The hearts for the Heaven.

29

God's Heart
Is our Progress-thrill.

30

My Lord
Amplifies and amplifies
My heart-cries.

31

My
Success depends
On my God-loving
Thoughts.

32

My
Progress
Depends upon
My God-surrendering
Will.

33

My
Surrender-heart
Becomes
God the Smile.
My
Surrender-life
Becomes
God the Pride.

34

My
Sleepless God-faith-vigil
Is indispensable.

35

My heart is desperate
For God's Compassion.
I am desperate
For God's instruction.

36

My soul
Is the Earth-discoverer.
My heart
Is the Heaven-discoverer.

37

My heart lives on
God's Compassion-tears.
I live on
God's Forgiveness-Smiles.

38

God
Loves my mind's
Emptiness.
God
Loves my heart's
Sweetness.
God
Loves my life's
Fulness.

39

God's
Compassion-Eye
Strengthens
My heart.

40

God's
Justice-Eye
Purifies my
Mind.

41

God
Playfully tries
To hide from
Our eyes.
But His Heart
Prevents.

42

A
God-faith-seed
Becomes slowly
But unmistakably
A God-treasure-tree.

43

God's Heaven-Music
Thrills
My heart every
Morning.

44

My
Silence-heart
Is God's microphone.

45

When
My heart cries,
God's Heart-Door
Opens up immediately.

46

Each
God-loving thought
Is as fresh as
A breath of dawn.

47

Come what may,
I shall run and
Run and end my
Pilgrim-Journey
At my Lord's
Feet.

48

God
Feeds my hopes.
God
Feeds my promises.
Alas, when
Will I be able to feed God's
Heart and His Feet,
When?!

49

May my outer
Life succeed.
May my inner
Life proceed.

50

To work
Devotedly
Is to walk very
Fast towards
God.

51

To-day's
Victory
We celebrate
Only to invoke
A new
Goal.

Notes to *My blessingful and pride-flooded dedication to the indomitable runners of the 3100-mile Self-Transcendence Race, 2006*

1. June 21st, 2006.
2. June 22nd, 2006.
3. June 23rd, 2006.
4. June 24th, 2006.
5. June 25th, 2006.
6. June 26th, 2006.
7. June 27th, 2006.
8. June 28th, 2006.
9. June 29th, 2006.
10. June 30th, 2006.
11. July 1st, 2006.
12. July 2nd, 2006.
13. July 3rd, 2006.
14. July 4th, 2006.
15. July 5th, 2006.
16. July 6th, 2006.
17. July 7th, 2006.
18. July 8th, 2006.
19. July 9th, 2006.
20. July 10th, 2006.
21. July 11th, 2006.
22. July 12th, 2006.

23. July 13th, 2006.
24. July 14th, 2006.
25. July 15th, 2006.
26. July 16th, 2006.
27. July 17th, 2006.
28. July 18th, 2006.
29. July 19th, 2006.
30. July 20th, 2006.
31. July 21st, 2006.
32. July 22nd, 2006.
33. July 23rd, 2006.
34. July 24th, 2006.
35. July 25th, 2006.
36. July 26th, 2006.
37. July 27th, 2006.
38. July 28th, 2006.
39. July 29th, 2006.
40. July 30th, 2006.
41. July 31st, 2006.
42. August 1st, 2006.
43. August 2nd, 2006.
44. August 3rd, 2006.
45. August 4th, 2006.
46. August 5th, 2006.
47. August 6th, 2006.

48. August 7th, 2006.
49. August 8th, 2006.
50. August 9th, 2006.
51. August 10th, 2006.

My Blessingful and Pride-
Flooded Dedication to the
Indomitable Runners of
the 3100-mile
Self-Transcendence Race, 2007

52

I offer
My outer run-results
To the Compassion-Eye
Of my Lord Supreme.
I place
My inner run-results
At the Feet of my Lord
Beloved Supreme.

53

My mind
Takes me out to show me
The world-market.
My heart
Brings me in to show me
My Lord's Heart-Garden.

54

Time knows
How to fly.
I know
How to cry.
At least
In one respect
We two
Are perfect.

55

To-day
The flames of my
 aspiration-heart are
Climbing and climbing
 to reach the
Zenith-Height.

56

I
Plan a long
Vacation.
God
Plans my immediate
Illumination.

57

The outer runner
Cries and smiles.
The inner runner
Sees and becomes.

58

I make my Lord
Supreme extremely
  happy when I
  claim Him as
  my own, very own.

59

Everyday
  my heart and I
  can love God a
  little more.

60

My God-gratitude
  is my heart's most
  precious treasure.

61

My Lord's
Silence-praise of
  my great achievements
  is most powerful.

62

My heart has only
  one task: love
God, love God at
  every moment.

63

There are so many
  ways to please God.
The easiest way
  is to SMILE at
  God.

64

A single God-touch gives the seeker
  enormous, ceaseless, unimaginable thrill.

65

Give not what you have.
Give what you are.
Soon, very soon
  your heart will
  become a
  twinkling star.

66

To think of God
  is good.
To pray to God
  is better.
To surrender to God's Will
  is by far the best.

67

Where is my
Lord Supreme,
  if not in my
  heart's streaming tears
  and my soul's
  beaming smiles?

68

Fear not,
God's Life loves you.
Doubt not,
God's Heart is all for you.

69

God claims me as
His own, very own.
Alas, when will
I be able to claim
God as my own, very own?
When?

70

My heart was
 born for
God-satisfaction-tears.

71

Each heart-smile
Is an
Enemy-conqueror.

72

Sincerity is the heart's most
 sacred song to please
God in His own Way.

73

To surrender to
God's Will is to become
God's all.

74

You can see God.
You can feel God.
But to describe
God is an impossible task.

75

God loves my streaming tears.
  I love
God's beaming Smiles.

76

God wants
My meditation-depth
To be the sweetest song
Of His Heart.

77

God
Is equally happy when
He builds and unbuilds
My heart-cottage.

78

To give is to
Become the king of the
Heart-Kingdom.

79

Only one Choice:
My Lord's
Compassion-Eye.

80

The more I love
God, the more I need God.
The more I need God,
The sooner I shall be able to please
God in His own Way.

81

My Lord, do you
  ever think of me?
My child, what
  else do I do?
What else can I do?

82

I am really happy
When I take this world as mine.

83

Happiness-seekers and
Oneness-lovers are
  very special to God.

84

God's affection is boundless for those
  who sing only God-melodies.

85

A true seeker lives between his mind's
Nothingness and his heart's Fulness.

86

I must never lose contact with my
Lord's Compassion-Eye and
His Forgiveness-Heart.
Never.

87

My Lord has a special fondness
  for two things:
My life of simplicity and
  my heart of sincerity.

88

My Lord's Compassion-Eye
Is my heart-home.

89

My mind takes me out.
My heart brings me in.

90

Aspiration-flames grow into the
Realisation-Sun.

91

God's Heart is the
Beloved Mother of all.
God's Eye is the Beloved Father of all.

92

Ultimately God's
Justice surrenders
  to God's Compassion.

93

The human in me loves to live.
The divine in me lives to love.

94

The happiness of the heart expedites
  the speed of the body.

95

Little by little I must
  change my life only in
God's own Way.

96

A heart of faith is a life of
  tremendous happiness.

97

The body is the patient.
The heart is the sufferer.
The soul is the sympathiser.
God is the Ultimate Curer.

98

Alas, every day
I do so many things deliberately wrong.
It is hard to believe that
  God still loves me and needs me.

99

The outer runner is a
  Hope of God.
The inner runner is a
  Promise of God.
The God-dreamer-runner is
  God's all.

100

Life is an adventure.
Be brave. Be victorious.
God is waiting for
  you to garland you with
His boundless
  Joy and Pride.

101

Be good and remain good:
If you want to be a supremely
  chosen child of God.

102

I love my heart-blossom.
I adore my soul-fragrance.

103

My heart-home is my
Lord's Compassion-Eye.

104

Every day I must strengthen and
  lengthen my love of God.

105

God remains seated always inside
  the heart-body.
Do not seek Him elsewhere.

106

God the Bird has two special wings:
Compassion and Forgiveness.

107

God's Greatness frightens me.
God's Goodness enlightens me.

108

If you do not love humanity,
You are bound to lose contact
  with God.

109

The Journey's start
  is Dreamful.
The Journey's end
  is Godful.

Notes to *My blessingful and pride-flooded dedication to the indomitable runners of the 3100-mile Self-Transcendence Race, 2007*

52. 18 June 2007.
53. 19 June 2007.
54. 20 June 2007.
55. 21 June 2007.
56. 22 June 2007.
57. 23 June 2007.
58. 24 June 2007.
59. 25 June 2007.
60. 26 June 2007.
61. 27 June 2007.
62. 28 June 2007.
63. 29 June 2007.
64. 30 June 2007.
65. 1 July 2007.
66. 2 July 2007.
67. 3 July 2007.
68. 4 July 2007.
69. 5 July 2007.
70. 6 July 2007.
71. 7 July 2007.
72. 8 July 2007.
73. 9 July 2007.

74. 10 July 2007.
75. 11 July 2007.
76. 12 July 2007.
77. 13 July 2007.
78. 14 July 2007.
79. 15 July 2007.
80. 16 July 2007.
81. 17 July 2007.
82. 18 July 2007.
83. 19 July 2007.
84. 20 July 2007.
85. 21 July 2007.
86. 22 July 2007.
87. 23 July 2007.
88. 24 July 2007.
89. 25 July 2007.
90. 26 July 2007.
91. 27 July 2007.
92. 28 July 2007.
93. 29 July 2007
94. 30 July 2007.
95. 30 July 2007
96. 1 August 2007.
97. 2 August 2007.
98. 3 August 2007.

99. 4 August 2007.
100. 5 August 2007.
101. 6 August 2007.
102. 7 August 2007.
103. 8 August 2007.
104. 9 August 2007.
105. 10 August 2007.
106. 11 August 2007.
107. 12 August 2007.
108. 13 August 2007.

APPENDIX

BIBLIOGRAPHY

Sri Chinmoy:

– *My Race Prayers, part 1*, Agni Press, NY, 2004. [RP-1]
– *My Race Prayers, part 2*, Agni Press, NY, 2006. [RP-2]
– *My Race Prayers, part 3*, Agni Press, NY, 2008. [RP-3]
– *My Blessingful and Pride-Flooded Dedication to the Indomitable Runners of the 3100-mile Self-Transcendence Race, 2006*, Agni Press, NY, 2006. [BDR-1]
– *My Blessingful and Pride-Flooded Dedication to the Indomitable Runners of the 3100-mile Self-Transcendence Race, 2007*, Agni Press, NY, 2007. [BDR-2]

Suggested citation key: []

Table of Contents

My Race-Prayers, part 1 — 7
My Race-Prayers, part 2 — 61
My Race-Prayers, part 3 — 115
My Blessingful and Pride-Flooded Dedication to the Indomitable Runners of the 3100-mile Self-Transcendence Race, 2006 — 147
My Blessingful and Pride-Flooded Dedication to the Indomitable Runners of the 3100-mile Self-Transcendence Race, 2007 — 169
Appendix
Bibliography

The heart-traveller

1. Aspiration-Flames — Aspiration and God's Hour
2. A Sri Chinmoy primer
3. Everest-Aspiration
4. New Year's Messages from Sri Chinmoy (1966-2007)
5. Flower-Flames
6. Songs of the Soul
7. Eternity's Breath
8. Meditation
9. Prayers
10. My Race Prayers

www.ingramcontent.com/pod-product-compliance
Lightning Source LLC
Chambersburg PA
CBHW030259100526
44590CB00012B/448